Contents

AFM History

About-Face Missions

a·bout-face

/əˌboutˈfās/

noun

1. (chiefly in military contexts) a turn made so as to face the opposite direction.

"he did an about-face and marched out of the tent"

synonyms: turnaround, turnabout, 'repentance'

The undertaking of About-Face Missions came about through a series of events that can only be attributed to God. A chance Facebook connection between two Texas based Christians, each having a passion for missions, resulted in an idea which one month later led to the formation of this group. David Shelton and Missionary Jim (abbreviated for security reasons) met in April of 2011 originally as co-volunteers for Global Media Outreach through Facebook, and since working in the same city, met for lunch – a friendship began.

David had been volunteering as an online missionary with Global Media Outreach for a couple of years prior. The Lord had connected him to an orphan teen named Ronald Mufebi in Uganda the previous year, who was surviving on the streets selling drugs. David led him to Christ. After observing how Ronald's life had been drastically changed by the Lord, and that he was struggling to survive without family in a third world country, David and his wife felt led by the Lord to help extend the love of Christ to him by becoming surrogate parents, putting him through boarding school and mentoring him online.

Ronald, 15 at the time, had a 19 yr. old friend in the gang, who was also trying to earn enough for school and survival, named Stanley. After Ronald had an encounter with God and met Christ. Soon he dropped out of the gang, in spite of the fact that it could cost him his life. Stanley saw the change in his friend and soon followed. He also gave his life to Christ despite threats of murder from the gang leader. As a result of dropping out of the gang, Stanley, like Ronald, was unable to continue school in 2010 because of a lack of money. He had yet to complete the 9th grade.

During this time, David mentioned to Jim that high school was expensive for Ugandans and that many of the children, orphaned because of HIV, were forced to drop out of school. This touched Jim such that he began praying about helping in the same way should it be the Lord's will.

Although Jim knew God had called him to help, he was unable to shoulder the cost of such an undertaking by himself. After some thought and prayer, God led Jim to post the situation on Facebook to see if friends would be interested in helping. In less than three days, a few Facebook friends had come to help, allowing Stanley to return back to high school and provide him with basic food and rent needs.

Shortly thereafter, the Lord gave Jim an idea and desire to move forward. He thought, *"If the Lord could orchestrate such a "miracle" for a youth in Uganda using Facebook in connecting people, why couldn't it be used to connect Christians to those doing God's work in real time?"* This led to the idea of *About-Face Missions, (AFM).* The Lord used this experience to amaze Ronald and Stanley's school administrators in Africa when they learned that a few Americans who had never met these boys were committing to help them graduate. They too gave glory to God in seeing this along with the local Church which the boys became members.

Jim and David Shelton partnered together in early summer of 2011 to form AFM ministry based primarily from Facebook contacts. The name came to them partly as a play on words since this began as a Facebook ministry. They felt strongly that God had called them into international mission work and to share the gospel, demonstrating the love of Christ, through helping the needy as they were able.

About this time both David and Jim had recently what they called a 'radical life-change' to give up the life of living for sinful self, and to serve the Lord with all their heart. Both men will tell you that they both had 180 degree turns in their life directions...an about-face! This is a military term that means to turn around. So naturally it made sense to call this new ministry About-Face Missions.

As the work grew and built more relationships with pastors in less developed countries of the world, they were led to incorporate in May 2013 as a Texas Non-Profit and become a fully functioning 501c3 NGO founded on the principles of Christ as seen in the Bible. Thus began AFM Ministry, Inc, doing business as About-Face Missions as recorded and filed in Dallas County, Texas USA.

Today AFM is helping those who are working in Kenya, Uganda, Philippines, Nepal, India, Pakistan, Peru and SE Asia through our continued support of former co-founder Jim. We have continued to utilize Facebook and the Lord continues to bring volunteers who are willing to go out and serve and those who are supporting those who go.

Interact with us on Facebook:
https://www.facebook.com/AboutFaceMissions

David Shelton is the AFM President, Director and Board Chairman.
Email: david@afm.ngo
Facebook: https://www.facebook.com/dshelton5
Website: www.aboutfacemissions.com

Our Mission and Beliefs

Our Mission:

Following Christ's commission to make disciples of all nations and extending his hand of compassion following the Biblical mandate to exercise pure religion of caring for the poor and needy especially the orphaned and widowed. We do this through strategic partnerships with missionaries and pastors in poor countries where needs are greatest, helping develop a strong universal Church all over the World.

Our Beliefs:

About-Face Missions is a non-denominational ministry. We hold to a traditional protestant Christian view of God, man and the Bible as can be seen by reading our basic doctrinal statement online here:

<u>www.afm.ngo/our-faith</u>

AFM Ministry has a more detailed doctrinal statement that we hold to beyond the essentials, yet we understand that there is room for differing interpretations in what we consider the "*non-essentials*". The above linked statement of faith, we consider the essentials of Christian faith.

Thus, it is possible to be a member of "*the Church*" even though you may not agree with the full doctrinal statement of AFM.

We welcome all members of the Body of Christ to join with us in prayer, encouragement and/or financial support of our mission to fulfill the call of Christ. Yet, every staff member or long term[1] missionary we send, or who we partner with to any significant extent, will be asked to submit to our more complete and specific reformed theological beliefs.

Notes:

AFM does affirm the Danvers statement on Biblical manhood and womanhood found online as well as the Nashville statement on Biblical sexuality and marriage. Both can be read or downloaded here:

www.cbmw.org

We hold that male leadership is the clear mandate of the Word of God and that women are not to be over a man in teaching or authority within God's Church.

Abortion: We believe the Bible teaches the sanctity of human life. We are given the precious gift of life from God and are created in the image of God. Therefore, we believe, in principle, that abortion ought not to be practiced at all by anyone. Life begins at conception and we should do all we can to protect the most innocent among us from willful harm, and we expect any who partner with us to hold to such a view. Our full doctrinal statement can be downloaded at:

www.afm.ngo/docs

---

[1] Anything more than two weeks

Our Ministries

Kenya

Mercy Children's Home

Jeff & Stephanie Bys Missonaries – Bungoma, Kenya
https://afm.ngo/mercy-home-story/

Our Mercy Children's Home is located in western Kenya. We launched in 2017 outside the city of Bungoma in the small village of Kaya. Jeff Bys[2] and family were commissioned to direct and manage this work for us because of the passion God put into them for orphans and the needy. As of Oct 2018 we have 85 orphans/at-risk children, 9 Bys family members, and our social worker living at MCH. We employ a staff of 23 workers who help us take great care of the kids God has given us to care for. Jeff also pastors a church plant that meets at MCH, Neema[3] Community Church, and he oversees a Bible school that also meets at MCH – in addition, he oversees several other locations in the area we call Sharon Bible Schools developed by AFM discipleship director Jim Clark. Everything that we do is intended to make fully devoted followers of Christ.

Pray about making a short or long term trip to Kenya, there is much work to be done here! Our future plans include planting more churches, training missionaries to unreached people groups of Africa, establishing a primary and a secondary school in Kaya, and establishing community services such as a clinic and police station in Kaya.

---

[2] Bys is pronounced 'Beese'
[3] Neema is Swahili for 'grace'

Philippines

Pastor Daryl
Mindanao Island, Philippines
https://afm.ngo/pst-dv

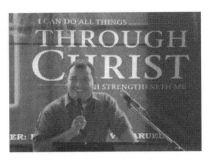

A vital ministry to reach the un-reached peoples with the love of Jesus among the war torn areas of the Philippines through serving the poor and needy children of the no-go villages of Mindanao Island

Pastor Christopher Samonte
Mindanao, Philippines
https://afm.ngo/christopher-samonte

Christopher Samonte, is an evangelical Pastor of Christ Blessed Family Church in El Salvador City, Mindanao Island Philippines with a focus on discipleship and church planting while serving the ultra-poor through food, clothing and educational compassion needs.

Pastor Romeo
Northern Mindanao Island, Philippines
https://afm.ngo/romeo/

An evangelical mission Church ministry to the poor of northern Mindanao Island among tribal natives of the area and to help local pastors train, develop and expand Christian discipleship among the region.

Pakistan

Pastor Munir Sajid

Khanewal, Pakistan
https://afm.ngo/munirsajid

Pastor Munir Sajid is a Pakistani Christian pastor active in evangelism, indigent children and compassion ministry, and leads a local congregation called New Horizon Church in his small Christian colony surrounded by hostile ideologies.

Nepal

Pastor Ram

Nepal – AFM Church and Orphan Home
https://afm.ngo/ram-babu-bk

An evangelical missionary church ministry to help reach the lost and make disciples of Christ in Nepal with compassionate care for the poor and orphans among this mostly Hindu land of many unreached peoples.

India

Pastor Manikumar
AFM Church and Orphan home in T Kothapali, India
https://afm.ngo/manikumar-gude

An evangelistic missionary home church ministry among the poor day laborers in India making disciples for Christ in rural Hindu coastal Muramulla village areas, and raising up and caring for orphans found in need.

Pastor Ganesh

Nirmal, India – Unreached tribal mission ministry
https://afm.ngo/nagavath-ganesh

Pastor Nayak Ganesh Nagavath leads a missionary multi-pastor ministry outreach in India to unreached Hindu tribes along with co-pastors in his BBC Ministry focusing on gypsy Banjera and Gondi tribal areas.

Pastor Sudhir
New Life Trust Children's Ministry and Church of North India
https://afm.ngo/sudhir

A Dalit-children focused, small Gospel outreach ministry to the poor families in Agra, northern India. Pastor Sudhir reaches the unreached Hindus of north India with the Gospel through compassionate material, food and educational helps, distributing to the poor families. This area has very little Christian witness.

South Asia

Missionary Jim
Unreached peoples of South Asia and 10/40 Window and USA
https://afm.ngo/jrb

A gospel minister working to reach the rest of the peoples of the world in the SE Asia region through mission trips to train the trainers, and to help develop more reproducible multiplying discipleship both here in the USA and abroad.

Around the World
Sharon Bible School and Tract Ministry
https://afm.ngo/sbs/

SBS is AFM's simple way to get some level of book by book, verse by verse Bible training into the hands of local indigenous pastors and their people at no cost, so that better Bible study methods are taught and more grounded followers of Christ are developed for Church leaders where little to no other Bible training is available for the poor. Also we provide free Gospel tracts by the case, for ministers and evangelists in these poor areas to use as part of their evangelical outreach work.

SHARON 🌸 Bible 📖 School
"I am the **Rose of Sharon** and the Lily of the Valleys"   Seeking His Abundance, Receiving Our Nourishment

Our Featured Ministry

The Bys Family – Missionaries to Kenya

Mercy Home Story

Surrendering the American Dream for Christ and Kenya

The Bys family sold all they owned, gave away career and savings to serve God as full time missionaries to help the needy. They boarded a plane from Texas in 2016 with 7 of their 10 children and headed to Bungoma, Kenya.

Why Bungoma?

The reasons are many, but ultimately it was through trips originally made by AFM founders who traveled on Gospel missions to work with various pastors in Bungoma. Jeff Bys, who went along with them, saw many horrific unmet needs that we all felt God was leading us to do something to help. The love of Christ compelled us. We saw how we could do much good with our few resources. In our desire to do the most good we chose this place.

In Kenya we saw receptiveness to the true Gospel and for us to come and settle there with such a ministry as this. As the Lord Jesus said, *"The fields are ripe unto harvest but few are the workers"*. We want to be faithful workers to deliver the Gospel message and through acts of compassion demonstrating the love of Christ. Where God leads us we shall go, and it seemed very clear this was the place God was calling us to go to be His hands and feet and heart.

Kenya has many orphans due to rampant disease and poverty. Disease, lack of education and poverty kill so many poor among them and it only takes a small amount to radically change that! The streets of Bungoma are also filled with over 250 abandoned young children struggling to survive and have become pariah to the Kenyans – sadly even to the local churches of Kenya. Few feel these street boys worthy to invest their time or resources, thinking them to be a lost cause. But we knew better! God rescued us, we who, like the Apostle Paul, were the chief of sinners, by the loving compassion of Christ Jesus – bought out from death to LIFE!

And this is His mission for us, so we go without fear, but trusting in our Mighty God to help us be his ambassadors of faith, hope and love, even to the most outcast of the world!

Jeff and Stephanie Bys
Mercy Children's Home Kenya
About-Face Missions
www.AFM.ngo/Mercy-Home-Story

Below is a Two-Year Rewind from a recent post from Stephanie Bys.

Today we arrived back home with our two visitors! It was an awesome day and we were blessed with easy and safe travels. Ironically enough two years ago today we were traveling the same roads to our new (temporary) home in Kenya.

We had no clue what lay before us but we were as ready as we could be. For anyone who hasn't been following our story from the beginning let me recap "quickly".

•2011 – Jeff began to talk about Africa

•2012 – Jeff was still talking about Africa and I was a "maybe someday".

• 2013 – *"Africa, Africa, Africa"* –Jeff

"Don't talk to me about Africa!" –Steph

• 2014 – Jeff started volunteering with AFM (About-Face Missions) and attempted a trip to Kenya, but it was bad timing so he wasn't able to go.

• 2015 – *"MAYBE, when all the kids are grown I will go to Africa so please stop talking to me about it!"* –Steph *"Hmmm…"* –Jeff

• 2016 – Jeff was able to go to Kenya with DC Shelton for 10 days at the end of April. While Jeff was in Kenya God made it abundantly clear that I was to go to Kenya as soon as Jeff wanted to. (I REALLY, REALLY did NOT want to move to Kenya – EVER, much less so soon.)

• May – November 2016 – We sold everything we had and packed 45 bags to permanently move with our 7 youngest children to Kenya.

• December 2016 – We moved to Bungoma, Kenya.

• January 2017 – Had the water well dug and started building our home.

• May 2017 – Started taking in children

• September – December 2017 – Many wrangles with the men we came here to work alongside with, forcing us to leave our home and we were even put in jail for a short time.

• January 2018 – We moved back home with the support of our village and our court case was closed.

• June 2018 – Purchased the ½ acre our home is built on. (Yes this was done backwards and we learned a lot)

• October 2018 – Finished the boys' side of the home and painted the majority of the inside of our home!

•November 2018 – Enough funds to purchase the front part of our land was donated.

So here we are 2 years in and I can't imagine living anywhere else. It hasn't always been easy and we have made mistakes along the way, but we have been SO blessed and learned a ton. We now have 90+ children living at Mercy Home, a staff of 20+, a church that meets here weekly and we have 2 visitors!

Thank you! Thank you for allowing God to use you in the lives here in our small village. Thank you for caring for orphans and widows. Thank you for building 5 homes for widows and families who need help. Thank you for allowing Jeff to live out his passion by sharing and teaching the gospel. Thank you for loving our children – I can't even explain what that means to me!

I'm crazy excited about this next year! We are hoping to open a school and welcome more visitors!

Come and see!

Jeff Bys is the AFM Vice President, Director of African Missions and Board Vice Chairman. Email: jeff@afm.ngo
Facebook: https://www.facebook.com/jeffreybys

Interact with us on Facebook at:
https://www.facebook.com/MercyHomeKenya/

"*Mercy Children's Home is an outreach of AFM Ministry's broader Discipleship and Church planting ministry to present and teach the world biblical Gospel centered knowledge of God (theology) and a Christ centered living of loving God and loving others.*

With that being said we take very seriously what we believe about God and his Word as it affects everything we do in some form or another and how we go about reaching, teaching and multiplying for the Lord Jesus."

— David Shelton, AFM Ministry President

Mercy Home Story
Surrendering the American Dream for Christ and Kenya
https://afm.ngo/mercy-home-story/

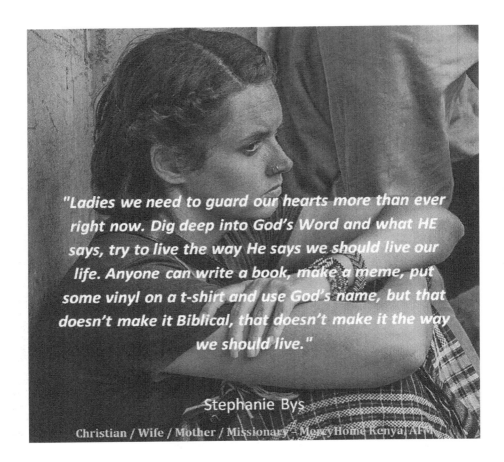

"Ladies we need to guard our hearts more than ever right now. Dig deep into God's Word and what HE says, try to live the way He says we should live our life. Anyone can write a book, make a meme, put some vinyl on a t-shirt and use God's name, but that doesn't make it Biblical, that doesn't make it the way we should live."

Stephanie Bys

Christian / Wife / Mother / Missionary - MercyHome Kenya| AFM

True Religion

"Religion that is pure and undefiled before God, the Father, is this: to visit orphans and widows in their affliction, and to keep oneself unstained from the world."
James 1:27

Trip to Kenya

Have you ever considered missions for yourself? Maybe it is something you have briefly pondered but never taken serious; or maybe it is something you have given thought to but decided against it for one reason or another; or maybe you are seeking where or what the Lord would have of you in terms of missions. Regardless of your situation, you should know that it is absolutely the will of God that we all partake in being missional. What do we mean?

First of all, there really is a true religion. James tells us exactly what true religion is. He says, *"Religion that is pure and undefiled before God, the Father, is this: to visit orphans and widows in their affliction, and to keep oneself unstained from the world."*[4] Notice that there is a *pure and undefiled* religion *before God*? Not only this, but did you notice that it is active in that it is to visit orphans and widows? Furthermore, did you notice that it is also

---

[4] James 1:27

to keep oneself (our own person) *unstained* (or unconsumed; untainted) *from the world?*

Keeping these things in mind, let us consider secondly what Jesus Himself says to His disciples, *"Go therefore and make disciples of all nations, baptizing them in the name of the Father and of the Son and of the Holy Spirit, teaching them to observe all that I have commanded you."*[5] Now if we only take these two passages of Scripture together, we would have this: *"In all places live holy unto God, helping the most-lowly treated people, avoiding the snares of this fallen world, and teach, preach, and call all people to come to the knowledge, love and true saving grace of God, here, there and everywhere, living set apart for His glory."*[6]

For in reality we are to be indigenous missionaries right where we are, and yet, we are to be about helping those who leave their homeland and serve other people groups. The founder of HeartCry Missionary Society[7] says it like this, *"You are either called to go down in the well or hold the rope for those who go, either way there ought to be scars on your hands."*

So would you consider taking a trip to Kenya and helping serve? If so, we would love to talk with you.

Some basic things to consider if you are interested in going over to Kenya are listed below. Obviously there are many more, but these are few to get you started

---

[5] Matthew 28:19, 20
[6] Author's paraphrase
[7] Although we are not affiliated with HeartCry Missionary Society, we do agree on the Gospel, the laboring for Christ's sake and helping to fulfill the great commission.

- Do you agree with the foundational beliefs outlined on our website at www.afm.ngo/our-faith. If considering a longer than two week trip, you must agree with our full doctrinal statement here: www.afm.ngo/docs

- Do you strongly believe that the Lord is the conviction behind your feelings?

- Are you cultivating a dedicated prayer life?

- Are you a member of a local Church with believers who will commit to pray with you?

- Are you harboring, holding onto and living in any unrepentant sin?

- Are you willing to provide 2-3 references from Christian leaders who personally know you?

- Why do you want to go? Emotions or conviction? Personal or others centered?

- Do you have the ability to fund the trip yourself or willing to enlist the help of friends, family or your local Church?

- How do you believe the Lord is having you to serve? Generally? Specifically?

- What timeframe are you considering? Sooner or later? Shorter or longer?

- Do you have healthcare needs that may not be available in a third world country?

Helpful Considerations

Prosperity? Seeking the True Gospel
FREE download:
https://www.thegospelcoalition.org/publication/prosperity/

When Helping Hurts: How to Alleviate Poverty Without Hurting the Poor... and Yourself

*Learn how to apply for a mission trip to Kenya – page 30

Indigenous Pastoral Discipleship

As a part of fulfilling the Great Commission, and a deep passion and commitment, Jeff Bys currently meets with 10 pastors on a weekly basis for discipleship, the study of the doctrines of grace and encouragement onward in Christ. Jeff has also been able to take men to several biblical conferences while in Kenya. This is an absolutely huge need in Kenya, and around the world, as the truth of Scripture, the realities of true grace and the Gospel is being twisted and sold as a bill of health, wealth and prosperity. We are hoping and praying that this grows in a mighty way over the coming days ahead. We need prayer, resources and men who will go out and labor for the glory of God, the sake of Christ, in obedience to the Holy Spirit and for the souls of millions.

How to apply for an AFM Kenya mission trip

The first step is to answer the key points below. Then submit your statements to us via email at: info@afm.ngo

1.) A summary about themselves and family
2.) Why they want to go on a mission trip to Kenya
3.) What they feel they have to offer to help out or what they would like to do
4.) Most importantly, describe their testimony in 3 parts
    a. Their life before following Jesus;
    b. What happened that brought them to true faith in Christ;
    c. How has their life changed, what difference has knowing Christ made in their life.
5.) Then answer the 3 questions below:
    a. On a scale of 1-10, how sure are you that you are going to be with God in heaven. (10 being absolutely sure)
    b. If you died and stood before God in heaven and He asked you, "Why should I let you into My heaven?", what would you say?
    c. Who is Jesus Christ to you personally?

Serving Opportunities

Mercy Children's Home Kenya

"Religion that is pure and undefiled before God, the Father, is this: to visit orphans and widows in their affliction, and to keep oneself unstained from the world."
James 1:27

About-Face Missions
afm.ngo/mercy-home-story/

The ministry opportunities seem to be ever so vast and open as never before, especially with the digital and travel age in which we live. It is so very true of what Jesus said, *"The harvest is plentiful, but the laborers are few. Therefore pray earnestly to the Lord of the harvest to send out laborers into His harvest."*[8]

Regardless if you can leave the country or not, regardless if you have little or much, there are opportunities galore. Below are just a few of our needs and projects.

---

[8] Luke 10:2

- Agricultural knowledge and skills training or consultation
- Daily Supplies – food, housing, travel expenses
- Travel limitations – need for a van(s)
- Medical Supplies and help – supplies needed, workers with healthcare experience, expenses for medicines and hospital visits
- School start up project: people with school operational skills to help us develop a solid Christian school program.
- Bibles and resources for biblical training – resources and men
- Church planting / Evangelism / Bible Teaching
- Care for the children – playing, reading, caring for and befriending the children / sports ministry outreaches
- Building skills and resources to come and consult on how to improve facilities and campus. We prefer to hire locals for labor to benefit the community.
- Outreach to the poor neighbors and widows – basic needs, food, shelter, being a friend to those who have none.
- Helping the Mercy Children's Home staff with their work and befriending them
- VBS type children's ministry help

Our Staff

AFM Ministry (About-Face Missions) is currently all volunteer staff since we are a small non-profit ministry trying to do the most for the Lord with the resources God has given us. Through AFM we have two USA sent missionary families supported, missionary Jim living in Tennessee and teaching discipleship methods, and Jeff Bys family living in Kenya overseeing our East African ministries. Below are some brief bios. of our staff and board. More can be read at: https://afm.ngo/our-staff/

David Shelton, AFM Founder, President, Director, Board Chairman
Email: david@afm.ngo

David is employed in the health care industry and gives his free time to oversee our ministry and reach more people for Christ. His professional experiences have been primarily in technical services and small business operation. David's passion has always been evangelism and discipleship which led him to foreign mission fields where he travels frequently working with ministers helping equip, encourage and spur them on in evangelism and discipleship. He served on evangelism teams with ministries such as Bill Glass Prison ministries, Needhim ministries, I am Second, and Global Media Outreach (GMO), as team leader and on-line missionary that focused on using the internet to reach and disciple people for Christ.

Jeff Bys, AFM Vice President, Director of Africa Missions, Board Vice Chairman
Email: jeff@afm.ngo

Jeff is married and a family man. He and his wife Stephanie have 10 children and lived in the Dallas/Ft Worth Metroplex. Jeff and Stephanie are now full time missionaries with AFM serving in Kenya with their 7 youngest children overseeing our Kenya Children's Home ministry and our discipleship ministries. He was prior a district manager of a food restaurant chain in the DFW Metroplex. He and Stephanie have big hearts for orphans, thus God led them to take his call for them in Africa. He has a gifting in pastoring the people of God. He has been a leader in his churches where he has served in children's ministries, youth pastoring, and as lay preaching pastor. He led a small church for a time as lead pastor and is firmly grounded in Biblical reformed theology.

Jeremy B. Strang, Public Relations Director, Board Member
Email: jeremy.strang@afm.ngo

Jeremy describes himself on his blog site, *"I am simply a Christian, a husband, and a father. I am merely a man seeking to further know and continue walking with my great and mighty God. I am literally a story of a stone in the making. Read more of my story, "Grace Upon Grace."* But we have come to know him as that and much more. Jeremy is also employed in the healthcare industry, but volunteers his time and talents to help this mission grow and thrive. Jeremy has a great passion for the Lord and a heart for missions.

Jim Clark, Discipleship Director, Board Member
Email: jim.clark@afm.ngo

Jim is a retired scientist but a lover of Jesus and the Gospel! He and his wife Donna have a long history of love for Bible study. Jim has taken many of these lifelong Bible study lessons and created an on-line school for the poor called 'Sharon Bible School' which is now part AFM ministry works. Through his passion to see people go out and evangelize and make disciples, Jim also developed a tract ministry to help get Bible tracts in the hands of the poor indigenous pastors around the world at very low cost through internet download. Jim and AFM partnered to work with our various ministers over the years and it only made sense to merge our efforts and unite under one umbrella ministry. So we invited and Jim accepted the position of AFM Director of Discipleship. Jim is continuing his work of developing and translating much of their Bible study lessons into local languages for our various pastors as well as his Gospel tracts and are continuing the Sharon Bible School a branch ministry of About-Face Missions under Jim's leadership.

Joel Toland, Financial Administration, Board Member
Email: joel.toland@gmail.com

Joel is mature in his faith, and leader in the Church and one who has a heart for making disciples for Christ. He is employed for a major airline company as a systems architectural engineer and is a active member of Watermark Community Church and co-leads community group with David. Joel is disciplined in his faith and in his life and leads others in both word and deed. He is both a sacrificial giver of his time and money helping AFM manage its books and a current consultant on the board of directors. Joel is married to his wonderful wife and theologian Holly Toland and lives in the Dallas metroplex.

Christina Brown, Administration
Email: christina@afm.ngo

Christina is a longtime supporter of About-Face Missions who desired to do more to help us in our calling. She is a homeschooling mom to 4 kids (all grown but one still at home) and happily married wife to Gregg Brown. Christina previously owned a daycare center for 14 years before the Lord called her to home school exclusively. Christina has served with Southern Baptist Ministries in Kansas City and worked in the inner city as a part-time missionary with children, teens and the elderly. Christina's passion in the church is people knowing the word of God and her passion is teaching the word of God, which she has done for years in various new-start up churches. Christina greatly desires that everyone comes to know the Lord Jesus Christ personally and experiences His transforming power in their lives!

*As of the time of this publication, no AFM staff in the United States, nor Jeff and Stephanie Bys in Kenya, takes any salary. However, with the growth of the ministry, this could change in the future.

**The indigenous staff at AFM Mercy Children's Home Kenya is paid a salary. This helps to support the local community in Bungoma, Kenya as well.

Final Thoughts

Our Chief Need

"Now Jesus was praying in a certain place, and when he finished, one of his disciples said to him, 'Lord, teach us to pray, as John taught his disciples.'"[9]

"In the days of his flesh, Jesus offered up prayers and supplications, with loud cries and tears, to him who was able to save him from death, and he was heard because of his reverence."[10]

"And He told them a parable to the effect that they ought always to pray and not lose heart."[11]

Without a doubt our greatest need, your greatest need, is for people to be a godly people of prayer. We need people who will, if they have not begun already, to cultivate a devoted prayer life with God. We need

---

[9] Luke 11:1
[10] Hebrews 5:7
[11] Luke 18:1 (2-8)

people who will be "*shut-up to God*"[12] alone with Him without the distractions of the world. We need people who will not only pray, but be a people who will be devoted to their God, being constantly "*transformed by the renewal of their minds*"[13] and set apart from the trappings of this world. We need people who will live out the Gospel, not only publically, but in their home with their families and in the most secret of places. The Christian life of communication with God must be grounded in humility as Christ our Lord lived and taught. Humility in prayer, in love and in service to Christ.

Although the best way to begin growing in prayer is to simply read the Bible, repent of worldliness and seek God in prayer, we know that often books can be of great value. Below are a few books to help you in this process.

- *Humility: The Beauty of Holiness* – Andrew Murray
- *The Hidden Life of Prayer & The Prayer-Life of Our Lord* – David M. M'Intyre
- *The Path of Prayer* – Samuel Chadwick
- *With Christ in The School of Prayer* – Andrew Murray
- *E.M. Bounds: The Classic Collection on Prayer* – E.M. Bounds
- *Revival Praying* – Leonard Ravenhill
- *The Lord's Prayer* – Thomas Watson

Eternity Stamped

"Lord, stamp eternity on my eyeballs."
– Jonathan Edwards

---

[12] Old terminology that refers to being set apart and devoted to God in times of private and devoted worship and prayer unto God.
[13] Romans 12:1, 2

"*Go therefore and make disciples of all nations, baptizing them in the name of the Father and of the Son and of the Holy Spirit, teaching them to observe all that I have commanded you.*"
Matthew 28:19, 20

28589481R00024

Made in the USA
Lexington, KY
19 January 2019